Good And Bad Relationships

A Book
by

Robert L. Harris

HATCHBACK Publishing
Genesee MI

Good and Bad Relationships

©2018 Robert L. Harris

All Rights Reserved. No parts of this publication may be reproduced or transmitted in any form or by any means, electronic or mechanical, or any information storage or retrieval system, without prior permission of the publisher or author.

Published by
HATCHBACK Publishing
Genesee, Michigan 48437
Since 2005

The views, opinions and words expressed in this book are those of the author and do not necessarily reflect the position of HATCHBACK Publishing LLC or its owners

ISBN 978-1-948708-28-9

Printed in USA
10 9 8 7 6 5 4 3 2 1

For Worldwide Distribution

Contents

1. Good and Bad Relationships...5
2. Honesty...9
3. What We Want...13
4. Great Expectations...19
5. Do Your Part...23
6. Stress Free...27
7. The Start of a Relationship...33
8. Divorce and Separations...37
9. Have an Open Mind...41
10. Things that Break Up a Relationship...45
11. Take the Lead...49
12. Inconsideration...53
13. Know who You're with...57
14. Surrender...63
15. Conclusion...67

1   Good and Bad Relationships

When in a relationship, it's either a good one or bad one. A good relationship may simply mean you get along with one another. You like each other and enjoy being together. The both of you realize how fortunate you are to have one another and you chose each other above all the rest! Because of this, each day may be just as pleasant as the day before. You are happy to see each other.

A good relationship only needs a one way ticket, the other, a round trip. You could be one of only a few that has it this way. You should consider yourself lucky! Today's relationships seem to have an intense struggle for one reason or another. Some are the silliest and some are the most serious. What goes on today puts a strain which may make it hard for people to come together and stay together. Sometimes togetherness can be a heavy load.

Sometimes we may not know how to get along. Maybe we do not know what the other one wants. And if we knew, we may be unable to deliver. Like anything else, being with someone takes effort. That's only if you want to keep what you have. Some people may not realize this, therefore, good ones are far and few. Do not be the one who doesn't know a good thing when you have one.

In a sense, it makes you look a little foolish. What you have is priceless. You have someone that takes care of you!

A poor relationship has few explanations. It simply means its not working well. It has no momentum. It crawls along the same as a snail. The bad between you brews just like a tea kettle. It's like a dull knife, it just ain't cutting.

To be in one that's not working is not good for either of you. You may prove to be just wasting each other's time. When you are with someone you really don't care about, the nights can be cold and lonely. Contempt may come up like the sun. You are not happy and may come up with all sorts of made up reasons to leave your home because you don't like being there. The relationship has no real purpose because it doesn't amount to much. Your days may consist of bickering back and forth to no end. Every little thing may well be reasons to go at each other. You may never agree on anything because you may not really like each other or it may be one-sided. You could be giving ninety percent while the other person is only giving ten. Someone may do all they can to make things work while the other is not receptive to any of it.

Honesty

When you are involved with someone, honesty really is the best policy. Many can't understand this even less abide by it. The truth is it takes a lot of work to be deceitful. One deceit may follow another and may take special efforts on your part to keep track of it all. This is not a good way to be because you may get caught in a small lie that may discredit you in a large way. When this happens, it's usually followed by lie after lie. You have to tell one lie to cover another. If you had trust in a person now all of a sudden it's questionable. Some are afraid to tell the truth because they don't know how the other might take it. In a sense, they may feel they have no choice but to lie.

A husband maybe too afraid to tell his wife the truth in fear she will not understand or she may leave him. So he carries the lie with him, maybe even feeling uncomfortable about it, hoping she never finds out. He fails to understand the inevitable, she will find out eventually.

It's uncomfortable to live a lie. Any second you may get caught. I'd be the first to agree it may not always be easy to tell the truth. Sometimes the truth maybe ugly but a lie may make it beautiful. Hopefully you are with someone who will try and understand. This may help you to be more honest.

You hear it all the time, just tell me the truth! Someone does this and now it's World War Three. It's a good thing to be able to tell someone what's happening with you instead of a cover up. What's even better is that you try and avoid lies in the first place. This can be a luxury to you because you really are a person that does not feel the need to play games and be sneaky. You are man or woman enough to tell the truth. You may even be admired.

Each of us may have things we try and keep to ourselves. There are possibly things we would like to tell and may have felt this way for a while. We keep things hidden because we may not know how to talk about it. Although this is not a lie, it's not completely being truthful either.

I'd say, the more you rid yourself of what

you've kept inside, you just may feel better. You have the courage to chance it that the person you are with will understand. If they love you enough, they surely may try. It maybe the insecurities we have in ourselves that causes us to not be honest. We are afraid we're not good enough or what we've done is bad enough. In order to impress or conceal, we make up stuff to seem different than what's really going on. You may live a lifetime of lies and cover-ups unless you are man or woman enough to understand you are something special when you don't feel the need to lie. You have the courage of your convictions and are willing to face it.

I was with someone that received a call and someone wanted to borrow money. He lied and said he was broke! I asked, "Why did you say you are broke when you're not?" He said, "I'm tired of this person who doesn't want to pay me back."I said, "Why didn't you just say you were not going to loan them money because they have a hard time paying back?"

That's the kind of honesty you should try and have. You are above lying, not beneath it. You have the courage to be honest. When you lie to someone, you lie to yourself as well. Any lie is simply a lie.

3 What We Want

No one can say definitely all of what someone may want. One thing is for sure, there are certainly wants someone may have. To fulfill someone's' needs may not always be easy. Although someone may do all they can, it may not be enough. The heart can be a lonely hunter. Some people are forever searching. They may not really know what they are searching for, and if by chance they find it, they may not know it. Some people are never satisfied. You can do all you can and it still may not be enough. It takes someone who knows better to be grateful for things done for them and to realize that someone cares. No one should be so difficult and complicated, that's if you want a well-balanced relationship.

You should try and keep your expectations so they are not too hard to meet and don't be one who expects perfect! Personally, I'd be afraid of perfect because they may want the same from me, which may go above and beyond my capabilities.

In my lifetime I've only known a few good

couples. Many people believe they want someone in their life, who doesn't? Everybody needs a place to rest and a place to call home. I don't believe anyone really want to be alone. Some people believe they need someone and feel this will make them happy. Maybe it will, who can say. Unless both people are ready and this is what they both want and are willing to do the right things, this may prove be difficult because there will be ups and downs. If you do not work together, it might be only a matter of time before you search for someone new. If you know you are not ready and you are not going to act right, be fair to yourself and the other person...don't do it! Do the friendship thing...the friends with benefits.

Believe this, people love and treasure all sorts of things, cars, houses, jewelry, and money. Why not treasure someone that's good to and for you? The saying is, 'Never look a gift horse in the mouth, they may shy away.' If you have a gift, appreciate it. This question maybe yours only to answer...do you want to be alone or with someone? It's simple! Do you or don't you? You may not have a lifetime to get it right. The young and foolish are so undecided. They can't figure out what they want so they bounce from one to another. What they have not figured out yet is eventually it may all play out. When this happens they will find themselves adrift in a sea of loneliness.

No one can tell anyone definite things on the subject of being with someone. It's difficult. You can't tell someone things they should already know. It's like telling someone that is grown how to start a car. We are on our own to figure this one.

Many people would love to be in a meaningful relationship. For someone that may want this, above all else, and can't have it seems ashamed. And if its love you are looking for, I'm going to tell you truthfully, love can sometimes be hard to find. Who doesn't want to have fun, be loved and understood?

What seems so simple can be so complicated. That's because people, over time, somehow get it so twisted. We have priorities that are mixed up. A man may care more for a car rather than someone that's there for him. Women may do the same. We can be so undecided and don't know what the hell we want, we may be afraid to give anyone a chance. We may be overtaken by all sorts of distractions that there is little trust and even less faith. As a result of this confusion, we have six billion people on the planet, way more than half are alone and some have given up all together.

A reason dating services have no shortage of patrons is because millions of people, both young and old, long for a companion that seems so hard to find. Someone who may live and work in New York that's surrounded by many people, you would think there would be no shortage of suitors. They can't find that special person even in crowded places, in hopes and a prayer, they turn to dating sights.

Think about it! You shouldn't take anyone for granted and feel you are entitled. Or maybe you have to lose it to realize it. No one can say to you stick with that person you are with. You are the one who has to read between the lines. I do understand people that are restless and so undecided. I can understand the confused state of mind. This maybe because what should be just isn't that way, things can be complicated. This maybe some of my own testimonial. As I have said, the heart maybe a lonely hunter, that means only that person may or may not know, what they really want. This is just another complication to add to the mix up. It's only one of many reasons it may be hard to find, maintain and enjoy the person you are with. Maybe for your own sake, sort it out, get it straight, don't get this one wrong!

4   Great Expectations

Some people have great expectations that may exceed someone's capabilities to please. This just might be that you are a little unreasonable. You are unreasonable to get with someone you know from the very start can't match your needs and you expect them to do so. It's like buying a mule and expect it to win the Kentucky Derby or buying a used car and get mad if it breaks down. No one can go beyond all they are able to do, therefore, you shouldn't get with anyone you feel they can't please you whether great or small. If you do, you really can't blame them. It's your fault, you should have known better.

It's best to be equally matched and have things in common. It maybe better if you both enjoy old school music or whatever else you have in common. The more you have in common may help cut down on disagreements. Things that you both may feel the same way about may help you to get along better. To be with someone who is more agreeable than disagreeable may give you a sense of purpose and add more meaning simply because it's an indication something is being said and done right.

Keep in mind, most relationships don't work because of the many different views each may have. This may cause the both of you to become frustrated with one another. It seems if you don't have the same views, it may be only a matter of time before the question arises...why am I with this person? If this takes years and you decide to break up, you may have just wasted precious time you can never get back. The only thing you got out of that ordeal was a bad experience.

We may not be able to find the one we are looking for, for whatever reason. However, consider this: sometimes someone comes into our lives that may not have all we hoped to find. Sometimes we dismiss that person because of this and it may be a mistake. I don't believe many of us may find *all* we want in someone. It maybe be foolish to think we can. We just might not be all they want!

I will say it may be how they treat you and make you feel. If you are fair to each other and the both of you realize you each may have faults, some hang-ups, and you don't have great demands, this may work. Many things amount to your logical way of seeing things. The problem...some people think they are so smart. They have all the answers. This can cause a person to overlook someone that could be right there for them. If perfect is what you hope to find, you possibly may be out of luck. Sometimes opposites do attract.

Ladies, if he treats you well, make you feel important, and he's not to self-centered and easy to be with, this may work! This maybe your guy. Fellows, if she's there for you, she's not a hell raiser and fault-finder, she listens to you, she really likes you, you maybe under six feet, but she makes you feel nine feet tall, this may work! She might be the one. Personally, I'd rather have a part of something than all of nothing.

Contrary to what some may think, there's good out there. If by chance it happens upon you, see it for what it is. Sometimes what you see in both respects, is what you get.

5   Do Your Part

In some relationships, the truth may be someone's not doing their part. Someone is dragging their feet that causes problems. Nothing can move forward as it should. There is little or no progress and you don't get along. Progress that should happen is not. The one that makes the efforts may eventually feel it's pointless to keep trying. They may not have much of a belief anymore. Hope seems hopeless, everyone is not happy, and life's no fun. Divorce and separation looms just above the horizon.

In order for anything to work as it should, each component of something has to function. Even at this fact, what should work perfectly can sometimes work with something that helps it to get by. This simply means, and this mystifies me, how can anyone that does not try to do their part expect anything to work? I do not understand this type of thinking someone like this has. It is like a kid still in the cradle that has no worries because mommy and dad are doing it all. Did someone not explain they must be of some help? Do they understand if they are not a part of the solution they are the problem?

In any good relationship, both are doing their part to make things work. This does not necessarily mean both are equal. One may make a hundred thousand a year, the other only half that, you can't expect the one that makes half to contribute to half of everything. The point is that the one that makes half contributes something. There have been many cases where the other had no income. Although they may not have had money they found ways to help. Something beats nothing any day of the week. You should not be involved if you are not willing to help. It's unfair to the other person. If you do this you may only be temporarily getting by. It may be only a matter of time before you find yourself looking for another home. Some homeless shelters are full of people that didn't want to do anything. I believe they wanted to cruise through it all.

It's better in my opinion to do your part. It makes you feel good about yourself. You should feel good knowing you make a difference. You have rights to your opinions and suggestions instead of like a kid standing around with a tootsie roll in his mouth. Ladies, help a man you feel is worthy because in a circle it may all come back to you. Any woman that does this may understand not to take a nice man who may need a little help and be afraid he's taken you for granted.

If you are a user of men, disregard. However, this is something you may want to consider, users sometimes run out of ways. While you are doing this you believe you fooling someone. You may even get away with it for a while but you are only fooling yourself. What you should know is not to ever grow old because you are going to feel the cold. You may find yourself lost and alone on a dead end street.

Fellows, pitch in and do your part. Do for her as you would want a man to do for your sister. Help her. You may find you accomplish more. Try not to be a drag along type of a guy. This may only go so far.

Have you ever had a job that was stress free? This made it not so hard to go to work. You may have enjoyed your job because there may not have been many demands that caused you to have tensions that kept you on edge. Getting through a day at work was not too difficult. You are a happier person because of this. You don't have the stress and tensions that goes with some jobs.

On the other hand, have you ever had a job where you dreaded going to work where your expectations were high and it kept you on edge hoping you are able to do all that was expected of you? You felt so relieved when the day was over. Once you got home, you were glad you made it through another day. If you didn't have to work weekends, you knew you could relax and put work out of your mind. You certainly were not looking forward to Monday.

The stress and strains of a relationship may be the same. Some people do this to one another which may make it seem it's not all worth it. Your enthusiasm may reach low levels. You can't figure out what's best to do. You don't know if you should abandon ship, or go down with it. You try and figure out ways to ease some of the pressure that is being put on you because of what maybe mistrust, false accusations, simply can't please, you're not doing this right, jealousy because someone looked at you, a suspicious mind that keeps you on edge, or maybe even afraid.

You could be questioned about time alone as if something is wrong with you when the truth is nothing is wrong, you just need some meditation time. You may even blame yourself believing that you are the problem.

If you know you are not the problem and just need clarity, here it is...what you may have on your hands is a hell raiser and a fault finder. You may have a small witted person you put up with. You have someone that's impossible to please and quick to tell you everything you do wrong. They never tell you what you do right. You are with someone who won't let peace be still. If nothing is wrong, they will conjure up something to fuss about. In other words, a person that's incapable of being happy and certainly don't know or even care how to make someone else happy. You may have a self-centered, selfish, unstable person you deal with. It's all about them! They may even be a tyrant. I hope I put it plainly enough.

No one should do this! We should try not to be this way! What does a person get out of making someone's life miserable? This type of person may be some kind of nut that thrives on unhappiness with themselves and others. They enjoy arguments. Either they get some kind of adrenaline rush or they believe it is supposed to be this way. Or maybe they just don't know better.

If misery loves company, be your own companion. This person is unsuitable to be with anyone. Who wants to be with someone that keep you on edge? This person may give you the feeling they are not happy and really don't want to be with you. You may not be happy since you have to fake it. This is only living a lie. Now you have frictions that simply won't work. All you get is bitter with the sweet. I guess a taste of honey is better than none at all.

It's so much better if you're able to say that magical winning word... Bingo! This is a winner. Instead of the other that is no good. If you put a hundred pounds on something only meant to hold fifty pounds, what do you think is going to happen? It's going to snap.

Who wants to be with someone that's hard to please? You always seem to disappoint them and you don't know from one minute to the next what might set them off. It's almost like playing with dynamite or being around an unpredictable dog. Don't be with someone who makes you have to explain every little move. You will eventually be forced to start lying. It's bad to be accused of something you are not guilty of, especially if you are not guilty! The person who is doing the accusing puts unnecessary pressure on someone to convince them that it's not true. If you have an attractive person you are with don't get the shock of your life if someone looks at them. Just as you were attracted to them, someone else may see it the same as you. You can't expect if you are with a good looker someone else is looking as well.

Try your best to have a stress free relationship. It's better for the both of you. If you don't like confrontation, don't you be confrontational! Stress is no good in any situation. It does seem ashamed to have stress from someone that's supposed to make you happy and make you glow like a hundred watt bulb. It's best if you are able to enjoy your peaceful days and restful nights, you maybe more content.

7   The Start of a Relationship

For some people, the start of a relationship may have been when we were teens. It may have been our first love? That is something to remember. Just going to the movies was special because you were with the one you were infatuated with. You may have even thought you would spend the rest of your days together. As time moved on, some things began to change, different things began to happen, like people, places and things. You are now looking at things from a another view. Father Time takes you on a fast ride and suddenly what once was is no more. You have become a different person with a different outlook. You may be ready to move on and leave all else behind.

Just as things like this happened back then, this may still occur in later life. You think someone would have learned by now. When you start a relationship its better if you know this is what you really want and be willing to do what's necessary to keep that person and make things work. People become involved with one another and sometimes for all the wrong reasons. Time goes on and they come to realize they have made a mistake, and they may want out. Usually when this happens, someone gets hurt.

Some people get with someone because they just don't want to be alone. Because of this, they are not as picky as they should be when it comes down to sharing someone's life. When this happens, it may be only be a matter of time before someone's not happy. Some people get together for security, believing their safe. If they don't really care for the other, this may not last, now everyone has to start over.

A relationship should be that two people come together believing they have found what they are looking for in one another. Each may not be perfect, but feel they are perfect for the other. To do it any other way may not last long. It is up to you and no one else to know what you want and to be in search of it. Sometimes to find that someone you want to be with may have the same odds as winning the lotto.

Things are real mixed up these days and time can be like a thief, especially if you are unlucky or undecided. A good relationship, I believe, is what everyone wants. Some people don't understand that if you are in one, there are things that are expected from you. There are things you must do. You now have a partner that may rely on you for things they didn't want to do alone. If not prepared and you are unwilling, don't get involved.

To get a relationship going can be hard. There is little trust and even less faith in people. Most anything can be a deal breaker. Some things should be deal breakers and sometimes we look for reasons to not be content. A man may have a woman who cares about him. On a scale of one to ten, she is a seven! He wants a ten. He wants perfect. He looks for reasons to be unhappy or maybe reasons to leave.

A woman may have a man that caters to her every need. She may see him as no challenge! Or she may be a beautiful woman with everything going for her that chooses the wrong guy that will use her to no end. That may have been the challenge she thought she wanted. It's no good just to settle for someone knowing you could never really be happy with that person. This won't last.

A reason why it might work is chemistry, this above all else! You should both like each other, love may come later.

When getting acquainted and you are considering being together, maybe come up with your own private simple test. See if they pass or fail. If they fail miserably, drop it like it hot! Almost from the start, ask that person what they want. Get quiet and allow them to articulate their thoughts. You just may get some of your answers, instead of waiting twenty years to find out. Asking and listening may help make up your mind.

8   Divorce and Separations

When people reach a point of separation or divorce, either one or both are not happy with each other. What brought the two of you together in the first place is no more. It's ran its course. It has reached a point where it's simply not working and both may feel its best to go their own way. You may have shared and had good times together and now its come to that fork in the road. It is important to make sure this is what you both want because you paths may never cross again.

If you know separation is best to do, try and bow out gracefully. Do not give each other a hard time because there might be reconciliation if either might want it. It's better to be easy on the matter rather than someone who goes crazy over it all. There may be no forgiveness if you've punched a hole in their tires.

When we get together we believe it will be forever. From the start we are happy with one another, this may even last awhile. So many things may go against a good relationship. Most anything can happen that disrupts it. The list maybe great.

If you really care and want who you have, the both of you need to beware, many things will test you. Give in to any of it and its over. Whatever it is, or was, has destroyed what you once had. Some separations are the best thing to do. Two people that just can't get along have an obligation to themselves to try and find whatever they feel will make them happy. It's no good to try and revive something you know is dead. Go your separate ways. That way you both have a chance to do something different instead of continually not wanting to be together and things may only get worse as time goes on. You have to face it when it is over.

If kids are involved, it may not always be so easy. Many people have stayed together for the sake of the kids. This has both good and bad points. It's no good to abandon kids. Although there maybe visitations and shared custody, kids may have an unstable feeling of being bounced around, not to mention they may not be happy their parents are not together. They may act out in defiance in anger of it all. They may have a preference for one parent that puts one parent against the other. Some kids may even feel its' their fault and may carry this burden. You may have an unhappy and angry kid that would much rather have his parents together.

On the other hand, when things reach a point when you no longer see eye to eye, separation maybe what is best. Who wants to be in something that's just not working? So if you are in a relationship, especially one that was once good that has reached the end of the road, when there are no new avenues to go down and one or both are not happy, living apart may be what's best.

9   Have an Open Mind

Both should try and have an open mind for each other. Unless you understand this, you may be sharing time with a stranger. A lack of communication is high on the list of not understanding one another. To not express is an unfulfilled feeling that something maybe kept locked inside. You may want to talk about things you want to share but you are either reluctant, afraid or unsure how the other might take it. This may cause you to feel you are not being the person you need to be and maybe unhappy because there are things you would love to talk about. The key to two people being together is to allow each to talk and express their feelings.

It's not a good thing to be with someone who you are afraid of. The other person may have shown at some point they had no understanding that may have caused you to shut down. It could have happened more than once and that's why you feel this way. We all, I believe, would love the freedom of expression. This may help you to become the better person you are, instead of being someone you are not because you do not really know that other person's reactions. It's like getting something that's half baked.

If you are the person someone is afraid to be with, you are possibly with someone that has great ideas or something interesting about them that's never known to you. Why? Because you did not allow them to express it. You are so quick to cut them off, they may feel there is no room for the two of you. It's really a one-sided. Are you in a relationship or know someone that keeps things to themselves? They will talk to a friend and tell them everything. They will talk about things they may want to talk to their mate about but they do not know how to approach them. This leaves the other in a place to never know about anything. So you are left with a mystery because you don't know the history of someone you are with. You are not a real friend in the sense of the word because you don't allow your partner to be expressive. You shut them down!

It's good to be with someone that has good discretion. The other person might think highly of you because you are someone they can talk to. Someone that's not so one-sided that does not always put down the way they feel. Your mate takes an interest in what's going on with you and allow you to be just you. This is growth for the both of you. You both may have better times together because you are friends that do not mind confiding in one another. Therefore you may get as close as you can to knowing and understanding the person you are with. To do otherwise, you are only getting half the story.

Being with someone who allows you to be open makes it easier. You may have had things bottled inside for years, now you are with someone who is supposed to help with that. The question is do they? Are they friend or foe?

If you do not, at least try and understand what you may want for you, which is someone to understand you, you should want that for the other. If not, it should come as no surprise to you if things do not go well in your relationship. Do not make that person that you are supposed to care about be like a kid who is afraid to tell his parents things because they are in fear of an ass whopping. This teaches a kid to be sneaky and may prep them to become a liar.

If you have an understanding, you allow a person to be who they are instead of someone you have made timid that does not know how to talk to you because you have not made it so easy. Being with someone who keeps secrets is like being with only half of that person. This is not good because you do not know what's really going on. You may be setting yourself up for surprises and the shock of your life. You may have only yourself to blame because this is one you overlooked!

10 Things that Break Up a Relationship

There is quite a list when it comes to all of the things that causes people to break up. For some it does not take much, while others hang in there to the last second. If forgiveness is hard for you, and there may surely come a time for forgiving, your break up may be easy. Some people do all sorts of things whether intentional or not. Some may not know better while some believe they may get away with whatever they are trying to hide. Once they are discovered, their mate is in for a shock. Some may put little efforts into the relationship and may not be there when they are needed the most.

There could be many conflicts in interest. Someone may turn out to be the one you thought you knew that has all of a sudden begun to act mysterious. This could be because something new is happening with them and you are left to try and figure out what it could be.

Then there is this word...compromise.

Personally, I do not understand the concept. How do you compromise if you buy a car, and you have your heart set on a red one and she wants green. If you buy the red one, she may get upset and says is all about what you want! The green means you didn't get the car you really wanted. What do you do? Should you both buy the color you want? To me this word means one is happy the other is sad! Try and have an easy compromise. And for some people, they simply want out, maybe for no good reason. I guess any reason is reason enough.

High on the list of reasons for breakups is infidelity. This one has caused many to go their separate ways. I don't believe anyone can totally understand why someone does this. A simple reason is they're just not happy. This could be reason enough. Some just can't be content with one person. They may have a high drive and just cannot control themselves. Some to the point of therapy because they feel they desperately need help. And some believe it's normal to have two or three different partners.

The understanding I have is many people are this way. What I don't completely understand is the why. Why has this behavior been put into people? Someone may have the best person in the world that caters to their every need. What do they do? They cheat on them! I'm not being judgmental. I have done this. For anyone who has done the same, try and reach a point where you are content with your mate. Some grow into being content. This is not the same as to just settle. They may come to realize its' just not worth it because they may already be in a good relationship. Then there are others who may be eighty years old and would still cheat if they only had enough strength.

   I understand some things can be hard to control. Someone that cares for someone may still fall for someone else against their own will. Devotion may only go so far. No one can tell you what you should do. To be honest, you should be a little careful with all of this fatal attractions and getting back at you type of characters you see so many times on the television. I know of a woman that tracked a man all the way from one state to another just to knock out his car windows because he left her to go back to his wife. Imagine that!

   In the ups and downs of being with

someone, don't expect it should always be easy. Many things may test you. It may come when you least expect it. It is best to look at things as they are or could become. You could live on a beautiful tropical paradise island for years and one day a volcano erupts that changes it all. Some good relationships share the same probability. Take nothing for granted. If it is working for you, don't be the one that causes the eruption. No one can tell anyone what to do. It's pointless to even try. Each of us do what we do whether it's right or wrong.

As for breaking up, only you may know that one. Don't feel bad if you can at least say you tried.

11 Take the Lead

Men are supposed to be leaders. A good leader is someone to follow. You believe they know what they are doing. One reason they are the leader is because they may know things you don't. They are appointed in the belief they will do a good job and lead the way for others. When you follow, you have placed trust and confidence in them. Whether chosen or elected, they are now in a position to lead the way for you. It makes a great difference if you believe and trust their decisions. This may help them to do a good job just knowing they have your confidence and support.

In relationships, men should be the leader. I would be the first to agree that all men are not, and not enough are. So why should anyone follow them? Maybe this is why things are so dysfunctional. Some men just don't know how. In a relationship, someone has to lead. Think on it. In everything, and function, and animal life, there is a leader. A man should be the head of his family because that's the way it was intended.

Not enough men know how to take on this responsibility, and some don't try! This is why woman, especially now a days, feel they have no choice but to take charge. It's not easy to be the one who has to make decisions all the time. Sometimes you become overwhelmed by it all.

It may be a luxury to you if you are spared this. You don't have the worries that goes with hoping you made the right decisions. Someone is doing that for you. This frees you to do other things. Whoever is more qualified, man or woman, let them have it! Back them up. If the man has good sense and doing a good job looking out for everyone, he doesn't have to demand respect but he commands it. You should admirer him for this. You may have that one in a million. Support rather than hamper him about every little thing. He has willingly taken on the roll. You didn't have to make him go to work. You didn't have to hope he paid the bills. If this is true, then allow him to be the character of that home because he's the overall character of you both. You have someone who is getting it done. Now you may spend extra time in the mirror, just to look good for him, instead of one who looks worn out.

Many women are head of the household these days. The man has either been kicked out or he ran away. Over time women have developed a belief they have to take charge. I can't say I blame them much, with all of the don't want to work, hanging out with the homies, chick on the side, other baby momma drama, laying around with remote control in hand, where's my dinner type of guys these days. What woman really needs this?

The demands on a woman to try and make sense of it all can be mind-blowing. Woman have been forced to do what they feel is needed to make it. This I understand, the only problem is that they may have done this for so long it is what they are used to. They were made to not rely on anyone. They may have relied on someone more than once and because of disappointments and a betrayed confidence, they may not want to believe or trust any man. That may come later in life. Since there is this no trust policy, a woman sometimes lose a good one. This is the shame of it all.

12   Inconsideration

Inconsideration for your mate is a reason to not get along. People do things and expect the other person to just understand, and if they have a problem with it, someone's ready to argue. When you are not thoughtful for one another you are being selfish and unfair. A selfish act on your part simply means it's all about you and what you do or want. Little or no thought is given to the other. You do things and do not care what the other person thinks or how they feel about it. It's no thought for anyone other than yourself.

To be this way in a relationship may not work well because the other may soon become frustrated. Once they come to realize their mate is selfish, they may began to feel not worthwhile because the other person doesn't seem to care what they think.

To be considerate is a manner of the type of home training gotten from parents and the amount which was taken. When I was growing up, to be considerate of others was like on the job training. It was like taking courses on manners and how to treat others. Over the years I've come to realize it's really intelligence on the part of the individual. This makes the individual a class act all their own.

There are things we do, and not think about the other person. It's wrong to be gone too long and not tell the one you are supposed to care about that you're okay. They may work themselves into a frenzy worrying and no consideration is given or care about how they worry. When one mate wants to do something that involves the both of them, it might be a little iffy when the other is not consulted. It's inconsiderate to be on a phone talking to someone and one mate puts the other on hold too long. The other call is not important.

Going it alone is what happens when a person shows from the start they don't care what their mate thinks or how they feel whether they have a problem with it or not. It's like oh well, go on with your bad self which seems to be the saying of today.

We sometimes may not realize what we do

to ourselves! By not realizing certain things, simple things that should be known may not work out well if there is a failure to understand. In the long run, a person may miss out. It does not matter who someone is, it's okay to care about what someone thinks or how they feel. A person who wants sensitivity for themselves should have it for others. We should treat people how we want to be treated. In relationships, each should have consideration for the other and take an account how the other feels.

13 Know Who You're With

When you become involved with someone you have now become involved in everything about that person, whatever it may be. You are now apart of someone else. The question is have you made a good choice? If you have, its smooth sailing. If not, it could be a hurricane that only takes time before it reaches shore.

Sometimes we may not really know the depths of someone and all the things contained within them. This maybe because they were able to make an impression. You became convinced this is the one for you. If its love, we all know love can sometimes be blind. It can turn out to be just a mirage.

People sometimes don't go beyond the moment when they think they want to be with someone. They may not realize there may be more than meets the eye. Therefore understand, they get what they have chosen if that person has a bad track record regarding anything. The key word is bad! If they don't believe in work, that's a track record. So don't feel let down if the other person doesn't get a job. When it is time for the confrontation about them not working they will say, "Ain't you working? Get off my back!"

If you knew from the start they are a gambler, don't be surprised if they lose the house payment. They may have a history of losing money. You may have known from day one a man is a womanizer. Do not be surprised if he goes after your best friend. All you've done was give him that easy access to her just because you are with him. This could be a reason some other woman dumped him.

If you have thrown caution to the wind, and you've made these mistakes, no one is really blaming you. There is no reason to feel foolish. This may be a learning experience. Take comfort in the fact you are not alone. Many, from all statuses in life have done likewise. Many, including big celebrities, have chosen wrong and lived in a fools' paradise.

The message is take time to get to know them. Do not fool yourself. Try not to disregard anything you know that may be a problem for you later. Know that you can't make someone over. They are who they are. That's it! Decide if you can live with whatever it maybe about that person, good or bad. Try and learn some history of that person. If they are a veteran, especially a war time veteran, they may have issues you may not see. Find out what they like and what tees them off. Learn what kind of temperament they have. See if you can understand their views on things. It does no harm to know a little about their family. This is because once you get with them you become part of that family. You will have interactions with them, this you can count on. Try and see if you can depend on that person or will they let you down when you need it most. A lot of this should help make up your mind. Above all else, once you have done this and you feel it may work, go for it. On the other hand don't believe it's something its not!

When a guy falls for a glamour girl he may have fallen for the glamour more so than the girl. He's in love with the way she looks and how nice it is to be seen with her. She has the look that makes everyone take notice.

He may feel he has found his queen. It should come as no surprise when she asks for two hundred dollars to get her hair done or three hundred dollars for a pair of shoes. If she has those long nails, don't expect her to do dishes. Her cleaning bills might be enormous. She may want a pedicure and manicure. If she's into jewelry, this could break the bank. Her want list may never end. The clothes she wears are not cheap. It's nothing but the best for this girl. Not only is her makeup flawless, it's expensive. To look like a million maybe all that matters to her, and she may expect you to pay for it. Since you fell for the glamour more than the girl, you wished for her, you got her! All that's left for you is to try and keep her in a manner she's used to.

No one should knock any woman for looking nice. Women should look nice. A good looking woman can make a man feel excited. However, there should be more than looks that make a woman desirable, just as there should be more to a man than money and a fine car. Look before you leap cause still waters may run deep. It's not so much what's on top rather what is beneath.

We should try and be with someone that

fits like hand in glove, instead of someone who suddenly scares you because of the many things you fail to realize at the time. You didn't see the big picture. Your eyes deceived you. Your heart and mind did not work together as they should have! And what may happen next...there's no telling.

So in the immortal words of a great singer, "Try and find yourself a bargain. Don't be sold on the wrong one. You should shop around.

14 Surrender

Many people in relationships are afraid to be nice in fear of what the others may think. They hold back on their feelings and what they may want to do or say because the other person just might get it all twisted. The other may believe you are weak and may take you for granted. This is so often the case. Why would you not appreciate a nice person? The truth is many don't. This may leave you confused wondering how it all went so wrong. All you wanted was to be appreciated an accepted for your goodness.

This maybe a reason why people are so bitter and don't trust. You may have started out and gave your all. That only led to being hurt and let down because someone turned your kindness into something petty, leaving you only to believe you have to develop a hard core attitude and maneuver throughout the lies, deception, and game playing many seem to want to do. Even this being the case, there are still some that believe there is hope they may find someone that's not this way, someone that does not take them for granted, who is not deceitful and don't play games with your heart and mind. They still believe in finding that someone who realizes they have who they want to be with and they may be the one that appreciates you in a way you've always wanted.

If you ever had this, you should surrender. The problem for many is that they don't know how. There's no real trust, or past experiences changed that. Whatever the case, you may spend a lifetime trying to protect and defend yourself from the game players. Overtime it may wear you down leaving you hurt and angry.

To surrender, many believe the word is to give up. To surrender to authority, an opponent or an enemy, or it may also mean to back down, cave in, relent or crumble. True, these are some meanings of the word and may sound like something we may not want to do. We think of the word as a defeat. There is another meaning and that is to surrender to the one you know that's good for you in ways you need to be treated. This person is past playing games, believes in them self and you. They have no bad intentions and care about your wellbeing.

There is no need for you to be cautious or apprehensive, that person doesn't make you feel that way. It's a relaxed state of being because you don't have to worry or concern yourself because you know that person you are with is happy with you. You know they are devoted to you, and you may not mind a surrender.

It's better to think of the word as something you want to do because that person has made you feel that way. That privilege has been earned. To give into this means it's unconditional because that's just the way it's worked out. There are no highs, lows or in-betweens the two of you. You are a part of each other, and both have given in to one another. It makes a difference if you understand this could be a good thing. You are lucky if you have this. Let no one tell you different, for the one that tells you probably wish they had it.

15   Conclusion

When in a poor relationship it's like being on a dead end street. You can't go further. If you are in a good one, it's like having a little piece of heaven.

You should know, it's not so much the monumental things someone may try and do for the other person. This might only be seen as you are trying to buy that person and this is not good. It is more about liking the one you are with and some things that are just nice to do. It may be the smallest of things that show you care and are thinking about the one you are with. This goes along way. A man may know what flavor ice cream his lady likes, and on the way home he stops and buys that flavor for her. A woman may know how crazy a man is about his tools. He tells her he lost one of them and she goes out and replaces it.

If you want to keep a relationship glowing know this, there are things expected of you. That person wants and needs things from you, otherwise they never would have gotten with you. The question for you is are you willing to give it a try? If not, leave it alone. You realize this may not be for you and you made an honest decision.

When you come together it is for all types of reasons. You want to be with someone that supports you and are there for you. You want that person to do things for you and with you that you don't want to do alone. What you want is someone that can make you smile. You don't need someone that keep you upset and crazy in the head. Life should become easier not harder. You should have fun together. Who wants to have dull times? Half of your problems should become more solvable. You both should know it's good to have each other. These are some of the things only if you are interested in having good relations.

This book has been about what we want, what we have or what we don't have. It is also about what we may already have and not realize it, and what may be a waste of time.

I've done my best to explain some of the things many have in our life, a partner! A partner maybe defined as a relationship between two people with coordinated efforts that has each other's back. Each are looking out for the other. They believe and think in similar ways. They want pretty much the same things and they work together to accomplish it.

A thoughtful nugget:

Sometimes a person may have a funny way of showing they care. They may not know how to express it. This just might be the way they are. Only you may know if they really do care. After all, showing someone you care should not be an all-out, exhausting effort. You have to know what's real.

I can only say if there is something there, and you are happy with it, it's probably worth it. Life is a game of chances. Chances are what we must sometimes take. Don't be so quick to dismiss everything. Some things may deserve a second look. I'd rather have a piece of something that's good, rather than all of everything that's bad. It's not so much perfection that counts, its sincerity that matters!

I thank you, and I can only hope that I've helped someone understand certain things about being together. I hope you have enjoyed what you have read. It was written in all honesty of my own experiences, both good and bad, and observations I've made over the years.

www.ingramcontent.com/pod-product-compliance
Lightning Source LLC
Chambersburg PA
CBHW071117090426
42736CB00029B/2590